Genocide Survivors, Community Builders:
The Family of
John and Artemis Mirak

# Genocide Survivors, Community Builders:
# The Family of John and Artemis Mirak

By
**Robert Mirak**

ՀԱՅ ՄՇԱԿՈՒԹԱՅԻՆ ՀԻՄՆԱՐԿՈՒԹԻՒՆ
ARMENIAN CULTURAL FOUNDATION
2014

# GENOCIDE SURVIVORS, COMMUNITY BUILDERS:
# THE FAMILY OF JOHN AND ARTEMIS MIRAK
### By Robert Mirak

Second printing, 2019
Published in 2014 by
Armenian Cultural Foundation
441 Mystic Street, Arlington, MA 02474

Copyright © 2014 by Robert Mirak
All rights reserved
No part of the material may be used or reproduced in any manner
whatsoever without written permission of the author and the publisher.

Cover & Book Design by
Arrow Graphics, Inc.
info@arrow1.com
Printed in the United States of America

Library of Congress Cataloging-in-Publication Data

Mirak, Robert, 1933-
Genocide survivors, community builders : the family of John and Artemis Mirak /
by Robert Mirak.
pages cm
Includes bibliographical references.
ISBN 978-1-4675-9766-1 (alkaline paper)
1. Mirak, John, 1907-2000.  2. Mirak, Artemis, 1915-2003.
3. Mirak, John, 1907-2000--Family.  4. Mirak, Robert, 1933---Family.
5. Armenian Americans--Biography.  6. Businessmen--Massachusetts--Arlington
--Biography.  7. Civic leaders--Massachusetts--Arlington--Biography.
8. Armenian massacres survivors--Biography.
9. Orphans--Armenia--Biography.
10. Arlington (Mass.)--Biography.
I. Title.

E184.A7M565 2014
929.20973--dc23                                                    2014000490

# Contents

List of Illustrations / *vii*

Introduction / *1*

· I ·
Origins / *5*

· II ·
World War One: The Exodus / *27*

· III ·
Settlement and Family: The Beginnings / *35*

· IV ·
The War Years: Alaska, California / *47*

· V ·
The Early Postwar Years: Halcyon Days / *53*

· VI ·
Tragedy and Trauma / *65*

· VII ·
Revival and Growth / *71*

· VIII ·
John Mirak, Community and Philanthropy / *79*

· IX ·
Growing Up a Mirak / *93*

· X ·
Fin de Siècle (2000-2013) / *109*

# List of Illustrations

1. Map of Turkey, highlighting the villages of Tzack and Mashgerd and the region of Dersim. / *11*
2. Bedros Mirakian. / *12*
3. Garabed Eramian. / *13*
4. Armenian primary school children in the village of Mashgerd. / *14*
5. Zaven, his uncle and aunt, Garabed and Anna Mirakian, and cousin Hovsep. / *40*
6. Artemis in 1926. / *41*
7. Wedding photo of John and Artemis, 1932. / *42*
8. Artemis with the four children in 1943. / *43*
9. John Mirak on the Alaska/Canada (Alcan) Highway. / *57*
10. John Mirak at the Red Rock Canyon. / *57*
11. John Mirak with Lewis (Lew) Warsky. / *58*
12. Newly opened showroom of Mirak Chevrolet, 1948. / *59*
13. Artemis with fellow Armenian American women. / *60*
14. Yukon Lodge, Oquossoc/Rangeley, Maine. / *61*
15. Vartges Mirakian. / *61*

16. 30 Mystic Street, Arlington. / *83*
17. The showroom of the "new" Mirak Chevrolet, 1984. / *84*
18. Mirak Chevrolet's new Service Center. / *85*
19. Side view of the new Service Center. / *85*
20. John Mirak with Set Momjian. / *86*
21. Jefferson Cutter House. / *87*
22. The Armenian Cultural Foundation, Arlington, Mass. / *88*
23. The Mirak family over four generations. / *113*
24. Bob and sister Muriel at Margahovit, Northern Armenia. / *114*
25. Ribbon-cutting ceremony at the Mirak Nursery. / *115*
26. Memorial stone of the Mirak Nursery. / *116*
27. View of Mirak Nursery in Northern Armenia. / *117*

# Introduction

The family of John and Artemis Mirak is well into its fourth generation. This short history of their family is a record of its vital statistics (births, marriages, and deaths). It also describes their characters and their achievements (and failures). It is written in the hope that the younger members and those yet to come will know their ancestors and the worlds they lived in.

A cynic has written that "Unremarkable lives" should go "unremarked upon, the way God intended."[1] To date the family has produced no Pulitzer Prize winners, college presidents, learned judges or Wall Street financiers. So, the history can be termed "unremarkable." Yet, in the very first generation, John and Artemis, two Armenian orphans uprooted from their homes in the old Ottoman Empire during the Genocide of World War One, began a family in the New World, acquitted themselves with distinction in a foreign land and set a great example of courage and achievement in their Armenian and non Armenian communities. These were no mean feats. (And believers in the gene theory of history can contend that the best is yet to come.)

Today memoirs and family histories are enormously popular, due in part to educated men and women entering retirement and to the ease of the computer. At the same time, with the increasing pace of change, information transfers, and a world in motion, adults look to their past for stability and psychological moorings. Whatever the conscious and unconscious motives, writers of memoirs and family histories are out in force. It is hoped that this work contributes to these new and important endeavors.

This family history relies in part on the work of sister Muriel Mirak-Weisbach, and especially the first chapter of her study, *Through the Wall of Fire Armenia—Iraq—Palestine From Wrath to Reconciliation* (Frankfurt, Germany, 2009). Muriel was also a careful critic and proofreader of the text. Dr. Barbara Merguerian lent her talents as well to a thorough reading of the manuscript. Dr. Ara Ghazarians, curator of the Armenian Cultural Foundation, ably translated the memoir of Anna Mirakian, *Verker ou Tzaver* (Wounds and Pains) (Antelias, Lebanon, 1960), and helped with translating certain Turkish terms. Alvart Badalian

## INTRODUCTION

and Aramais Andonian of Arrow Graphics helped in the final product, while daughter Julia Mirak Kew assisted in selecting the photos. And she, her sister, Dr. Jennifer Mirak Leach, and their families—as well as those who preceded them—inspired me to complete this work. I am grateful to them all.

---

[1] Neil Genzlinger, *New York Review of Books*, May 12, 2011.

· I ·

# Origins

The modern history of our family begins in the cataclysmic days of World War One. In 1915 our parents-to-be, Zaven Mirakian and Artemis Eramian, were eight years old and one year old respectively. For no reason of their causing, their worlds were turned upside down. It is a wonder they survived. It is also a testament to extraordinary love and extraordinary strength that they matured, made their ways to the New World, and started our family.

Let us begin with Zaven Mirakian, who became John Mirak. He was born in 1907 in the tiny village of Mashgerd, near the town of Arabkir, in the Turkish Armenian province of Mamuret-Ul-Aziz. DNA records trace Zaven's ancestors (and ours) back 250,000 years, and to Africa and the birth of our species. As the saying goes, "Every journey began in Africa." And successive migrations took those distant generations through the Middle East, across the Caucasus Mountains and eventually to the Anatolian plateau (now Turkey).[1]

But this is the remote past, which remains to be explored. The first records of Zaven's ancestors are from 1750. In that year, according to a family tree, Zaven's predecessors left their historic home in the mountains and valleys of Dersim, a wild and untamed hinterland of the Ottoman Empire, crossed the mighty Euphrates River, and settled in the village of Mashgerd.[2] According to a later Ottoman census, the Mirakians of Dersim were numerous, some 7,000 in all.[3] As such they formed the paramount Christian clan in its villages. Like the numerous neighboring Kurdish tribes, they lived off the land, as shepherds, keeping "thousands of goats and sheep," whose products gave them food and clothing. Industrious, tied to the land, they were also indispensable defenders of their homes. With great prowess in fighting (they were master horsemen proficient with rifles and swords), they allied with neighboring Kurdish tribes in frequent, successful fights against the encroachment of Turkish armies. At any one time the Mirakians could put 3,000 warriors into the battlefield; and in one encounter, when their Kurdish allies deserted them, the clan called on its trusted and capable women and boys for help. According to one source, the name "Mirakian" created fear and

# I. ORIGINS

trembling in the ranks of Turkish soldiers. Indeed, much of the military history of the region is their story. And their renown was so great that the name "Mirak," which comes from the Kurdish "Miro"—lord or prince—was bestowed on them by their Muslim neighbors as a sign of immense respect and admiration.

Although until modern times the Mirakians were uneducated and also had no local churches of their own, they were faithful to their Armenian religion, abiding by the sacred rites of the historic Christian church.

The final dispersion of the clan from Dersim began with the atrocities of the Russo-Turkish war of 1877-78 and intensified with the Armenian massacres of the 1890s. The clan was now scattered through the Ottoman Empire and elsewhere. By this time three generations of Mirakians had settled in the province of Mamuret-Ul-Aziz in the locality of Arabkir and the village of Mashgerd. Except for the family tree, there is no specific evidence of the date of the migration, but only of the fact that it occurred. This issue remains to be researched. However, for those who believe in the role of genes in history and those who knew him personally, there is no doubt that Zaven Mirakian, the male founder of our modern family, came from the illustrious bloodlines of the renown Mirakian clan of Dersim.

Our first glimpses of Zaven as a child and his family come from two remarkable photographs. The first, of his father Bedros, probably in his late 30s, depicts a handsome, forceful presence, with a high forehead and a clear gaze. As the oldest of his siblings, he probably offered sage advice and guidance. For example, when his younger brother Garabed left Mashgerd for America in 1912 it was likely with his older brother's encouragement. The second photograph is from around 1913 and is of Zaven, his classmates, and his instructor at the village Armenian school.

Physically he is smaller than many of the other children. His dreamy expression, which followed him throughout his life, masks (as we shall see) a forceful mind and character. He is holding a Bible and is dressed in a velvet finished coat, probably reflecting the family's status as prominent artisans (tailors) in the village.

Zaven's village numbered 600 dwellings.[4] Built at some height and blessed with ample orchards and springs, it was, as Zaven remembered years later, "beautiful." There he lived with his parents, a grandmother, and in time younger siblings, Vartges and Yeprad (Euphrates), so named because Mashgerd lay near the confluence of three rivers, including the majestic Euphrates.

# I. ORIGINS

In November 1895 Mashgerd was decimated by the first of the modern massacres by Turks, but it was rebuilt, in part through benefactions from survivors who had fled to Aleppo, Cairo, and the United States. Its final destruction took place in 1915, in the genocide of World War One. Zaven and his brother Vartges were the only family members to survive. How and why they escaped comes from Zaven's pen and from a moving account by Zaven's aunt, Anna Mirakian, a story to which we shall soon return.

Artemis Eramian, the female founder of our modern family, was born in 1914[5], as World War One was breaking out. Her birthplace was also in the Turkish Armenian province of Mamuret-Ul-Aziz, near the town of Arabkir and in the tiny village (100-150 homes) of Tzack.[6] Like so many other Armenian villages, it was built against a hillside, amid lush fields and ample springs. As was the pattern in the Ottoman Empire, the village was a center of Armenian artisans—shoemakers, ironworkers, watchmakers, bakers, carpenters—whose products were exchanged for the agricultural harvests of its six surrounding Turkish villages. Stirred by the educational awakening of Armenians in Turkey in the nineteenth century, it boasted schools for Armenian boys and girls—as well as Turkish students in their own language and literature—and sent its young people to colleges in Kharpert, Constantinople, and elsewhere. As the crow flies, Tzack was five miles from Mashgerd, Zaven's village, but Artemis's family and Zaven's family did not know each other in the Old Country before the Genocide.

In Tzack, Artemis was an only child who lived with her mother, Mariam. Her father, Garabed, had emigrated to the United States around 1895 and had returned in 1910 to his village, perhaps to persuade his parents to leave for America. (Her parents' families were landowners in the village and her paternal grandfather was a successful moneylender who convinced his son to remain in the Old Country and raise a family. Garabed was also a man of means, who had invested in Egyptian bonds.)[7]

**WORLD WAR ONE: THE ABYSS**

During World War One Zaven's and Artemis's stories were strikingly similar: each was orphaned; each was saved by Turkish families; each was rescued by a heroic relative and brought to the New World. But the details of their odysseys are so dramatic and different that each requires a separate telling.

*Artemis's story.* In 1915, Artemis's village and Zaven's village were put to the sword. World War One had broken

1. Map of Turkey, highlighting the villages of Tzack and Mashgerd and the region of Dersim.

2. Bedros Mirakian, father of Zaven Mirakian (John Mirak). Died in the Genocide of 1915.

3. Garabed Eramian, father of Artemis Eramian. Also died in the Genocide of 1915.

4. Armenian primary school children in the village of Mashgerd. Only the children marked with x's survived the Genocide. Zaven Mirakian is in the back row, the sixth from the right. He is apparently holding a Bible.

# I. ORIGINS

out, and the Turkish government (under the ruling Young Turks) determined to eradicate the Armenian presence in Turkey. The Armenians, a Christian minority in a Muslim state, wealthier than their neighbors, suspected as allies of the enemy Russians and impediments to a pure Turkish state—Turkey for the Turks—became victims of the first Genocide of the Twentieth Century.

Artemis's striking account, written years later, of the massacres in Tzack, her rescue and early upbringing by a Turkish family, and her eventual reunion with Armenian relatives is worth quoting at length.[8]

*I was just an infant when the mass killings began, 1915-1916. Our village people were gathered in the church hall, all the men, women, and children were kept there for days. Then the gendarmes, the Turkish soldiers, took groups at a time, to a distance of five or ten miles, and shot them to death. My mother, my grandmother, and other women, and children were grouped, and shot to death. My mother held me, her infant baby, Artemis, to her breast, so that the baby would die with her. But the bullet missed me. . . .*

*A few days later, a Turkish shepherd grazing his sheep, heard an infant crying among the dead bodies. He picked up the little infant and carried her, and left her on the steps of a Turkish mosque. I don't know for how many days this infant was left outdoors. Then, one day came a gendarme of this town, called Omar. He took pity, seeing this infant, and carried her home and asked his wife, Gulnaz, to take her in. They had no children. She refused to take her in, she was not going to take care of a "giavour" child, a Christian, and she said she was too old to take care of an infant. Finally, she consented to keep her overnight.*

*The next morning, she took the child and left her at the [mosque] doorstep. While talking with her neighbors, sitting there, what happened was, the little one crawled over to her and held onto her skirt. Right then and there, tears came to Gulnaz's eyes, and she vowed that Allah had sent this child to her, and that she would love me and care for me as long as she lived. They named me Noveria, and I was known by that name.*

*She loved me dearly, and I grew up and called her "Anna," which means "mother" in Turkish. I had the best of everything: beautiful clothes—I was the only baby who wore red buckled shoes—and the best of food. . . . I spoke only Turkish. I remember at dinner time, that is the evening meal, the "Kazah" would sing the evening prayer from the minaret, and then we would start to eat our meal. This was a ritual.*

I. ORIGINS

*I didn't know I was an Armenian child, they kept it secret from me. Then, about 1917, or so, the Armenians who had survived returned to their homes. There was nothing left but bare walls. In order to live, some of these women went out to the Turkish homes to do housework, and get food in return. It happened that one of my aunts, Margret Dedekian, came to our house. She recognized me immediately, but Gulnaz Hanim [Madam] at first denied that I was an Armenian child. Then, after a fashion, she told the ladies how she found me. She showed them the little pinafore dress, all stained with blood, and my silver bracelet. There was a warm friendship between these ladies. My relatives did their housework, and went home happy, knowing that I, too, was alive, and well taken care of. They went back to their village and told my cousin, Joovar Millian, that Artemis was alive, and living with a Turkish family.*

*Shortly after 1917, the Armenians who had survived the Genocide were allowed to travel freely. My cousin Joovar came to visit me, but I did not know who she was. I remember being very shy and uneasy being with her. You see, I had been told I was Turkish and she was "giavour." She made many visits, it was quite a distance. She walked all day to make the trip. She did not have a horse or buggy, she just walked all day, just to come to see me. Joovar's father and my father were brothers. Her father had died and she lived with her mother and grandmother. My cousin Joovar had no children of her own. She had taken in an orphaned half-sister Siranoush, [and] Boghos, a nephew of her husband, and lived in the house in Tzack village. She had lots of farmland, which belonged to her family and mine, with vineyards. Her husband was in America, but she had no communication with him until 1918 or 1920.*

*One day I was playing with the children, and I came home to find lots of people in our house, and I wanted to know why. My father, the Turkish gendarme, Omar, had taken ill and died suddenly. To this day, I remember all the village people coming, crying, the old people huddled together in grief. I was crying too. I had no father to take me horse-back riding or buy me pretty clothes. What was to become of me? But I had my Anna, who loved me more than ever. She was a very warm and loving person, always cuddling me, always looking after my needs. I loved her dearly. My Anna, my mother.*

*Shortly thereafter, maybe a year or so, my mother married a young Turkish soldier, handsome, and much younger than her first husband, Omar. Gulnaz Hanim*

## I. ORIGINS

*was a wealthy widow so this young man married her for her wealth. He had another wife and children. In those days, the Turkish men were allowed to have more than one wife.*

*Perhaps a year or so passed. My cousin still visited me, and they were all on friendly terms. When Omar was alive, he had warned my cousin Joovar, she should never, never think of taking me away from him: he would have killed her instantly. His warning didn't scare her, she kept coming as often as possible. When he died, things changed. The new husband of Gulnaz didn't care about me, as he had children of his own. They talked it over with my cousin Joovar. If she wanted me, she could have me.*

*Also at that time, the Turkish government passed a new law saying, if there were any Armenian children living with Turkish families, they should be returned to their Armenian relatives—mothers, sisters, brothers, or cousins—who would claim them rightfully by law. This was in good faith; out of all evil, some good comes.*

*So my Anna dressed me up in pretty clothes, a beautiful silk dress and red shoes. She and her husband took me to Tzack village. We rode on horseback. I rode in the front of the saddle with my mother and her new husband led us. I don't remember how long a journey it was. We reached the village at dusk, and it happened to be the day before Easter. All the people in the village came to welcome us, with home-made goodies, cheoreg bread, cheese, eggs and Kharma, cooked lamb. We had a great dinner. What a celebration! Everyone here was Armenian, and I could not understand one word of Armenian.*

*The next morning, my Anna and her husband left, for Agin, their home town. I cried and cried after them. I wanted to go back with them. I stayed. I had to. The only person I knew here was Joovar Ablah, my cousin. I held onto her wherever she went. There was Siranoush (her half-sister), a couple of years older than I, and Boghos, the nephew of her husband.*

*Siranoush did not like me, she used to call me "Turk" because I did not speak Armenian. Within six months or so, I began to learn to speak Armenian. We went to an Armenian school in the village and I made many friends there. . . . In this village, there were only women and children, no men. I never remember seeing a wedding or a new-born baby. We who survived were orphans of the massacre.*

*Zaven's story.* Such was Artemis's story. We turn now to Zaven, and two powerful accounts of his experiences through the Genocide.

## I. ORIGINS

The first of these accounts is a two-page letter by Zaven (now John Mirak) in the late 1980s, to Professor Justin McCarthy, a well known apologist for the Turks and denier of the Genocide.[9] In it John Mirak forcefully challenges McCarthy's whitewashing of the massacres. The second is by Zaven's aunt, Anna Mirakian. Entitled *Wounds and Pains,* it is an engrossing sixty-page Armenian language account, written in the 1960s, of her wrenching experiences during the Genocide: ("I dedicate this memoir of a heartbroken and inconsolable mother to her children Eghsapet, Avedis and Hovsep. They were lost in the thorny path, and they may perhaps even be alive and living among the nomads of northern Syria. But if they are dead, let the tears shed by their grieving mother turn into drops and shower their graveless remains like morning dew.")[10]

Of our three witnesses to the Genocide—Anna Mirakian, Zaven, and Artemis—Anna Mirakian, already an adult at the time, was well-educated. According to her account, she was born in 1889, in the cosmopolitan city of Aleppo, Syria, to a family of tailors and attended local Armenian schools and the Armenian Catholic nuns school, specializing in French and embroidery. In 1904 she married Garabed Mirakian—Zaven's uncle—and then moved first to the more remote village of Mashgerd, which stultified her lively mind and personality, and then to the larger town of Arabkir. She and Garabed had three surviving children before Garabed left in 1912 for the United States to avoid entanglement with Turkish authorities who were drafting Armenians into the Turkish military. When World War One broke out, she was living with her children in Mashgerd.

The massacres which left Artemis an orphan in Tzack in the fall of 1915 were part of a larger assault on the Armenian communities in the Arabkir region. The village of Mashgerd, the home of Zaven's family and that of his aunt, Anna Mirakian, was not spared. Writing years later, Zaven recounted:

*My family residence was a village near Arabkir. As there are many villages in the surrounding area, in 1914 a large plaque was hung up in the center of the town, which meant that the Turkish government was at war approximately six months later. All the Armenians were told to surrender their weapons so there would be peace in our area, and the Armenians obeyed this order. Some time had passed; approximately 1915 a group of Turkish soldiers on horses entered the village and rounded up all the able-bodied men, including my father, the priests, the teachers, bound their hands and marched them out of the village, about ten miles, next to the Euphrates River.*

# I. ORIGINS

*They killed some and drowned the rest. This was called the First Massacre.*

*The Second Massacre took place about six months later. They took all boys, girls, and women 12 years or older, about four miles out of town and killed them. My family and my cousins were included.*

*The Third Massacre took place approximately in the middle of 1916. It included all the old people, men and women, and children. They gathered them and locked them in the church for four days and on the fifth day, they brought them to the center of the town. I then ran to my house, which was about 100 yards away. As you entered the house, my grandmother was lying on a couch, she was very ill. I ran in the back stable to hide. I then heard Topal Nury come and ask my grandmother where I was. She told him she had not seen me, he then left. Topal Nury was the chief executioner of the whole region of that part of the Turkish province. "Topal" in Turkish means "lame," so it must have been a nickname.*

*The final massacre took place less than a mile outside of town. Because of their inability to walk any further, they were all killed there. Approximately a month later, I was near the village square with our neighbor, a Turkish woman. Topal Nury arrived on a horse and he grabbed me and shouted, "You were the one who escaped." Then the Turkish woman looked at him and shouted back, and said, "Haven't you killed enough? Why don't you leave the boy alone to care for his grandmother, who is dying, and his young infant brother?" So he left me alone. Within a week, my grandmother died. I asked the lady's husband if he would help me bury her, and he was kind enough to dig a grave in our land and bury her. A week later, I went to him again to bury my brother, who was less than a year old and had died from starvation. I was the only Armenian left in the village. Another kind Turkish woman who felt sorry to me gave me shelter and food, and I worked for her for a few months.*

So, like Artemis, Zaven had lost his family to the Turkish executioners. And like Artemis, he had been saved by compassionate Turks.

---

[1] In seeking the genealogy of the Mirak family, the author consulted the Armenian DNA Project (part of Family Tree DNA—Genealogy by Genetics, Ltd.) His sample DNA yielded two results: a) that no one in the Armenian DNA database "is even remotely close to you" and b) "your maternal haplogroup [branch of the human genetic tree] is both very ancient and rooted in the Anatolia/Caucasus region." The information about the human species is common knowledge. For the early history of the Armenians, see Richard Hovannisian, ed., *The Armenian People from Ancient to Modern Times* (New York, 1997),Vol. I, chapters I and II.

## I. ORIGINS

[2] The family tree is entitled "The Genealogy of Mirakian Family From 1750 to 1990s" and was constructed by Diran Chorabanian, a close family friend.

[3] An extensive discussion of the Mirakian clan is in K. A. Yerevanian, *Badmutiun Charsanjaki Hayots* [History of the Armenians of Charsanjak] (Beirut, 1956).

[4] A too brief description of Mashgerd is in Antranig Poladian, *Badmutiun Hayots Arabgeri* [History of the Armenians of Arabkir] (New York, 1960).

[5] Although Artemis Eramian believed she was born in 1915, her birth date is more likely a year earlier, so that when the massacres swept through her village in mid 1915, she was close to a year old. Artemis's maiden name on her passport to America was "Eramian," although in later years she used "Yeramian."

[6] Unlike Mashgerd, the sources for Tzack are unusually rich. See Poladian, *Badmutiun,* Hovhannes M. Kehayian *Arabgeri Tzack–Kiughi Gianken,* [The Life of Arabkir's village, Tzack] (Beirut, 1956) and Sarkis Dedekian, *Memoirs Zak Village,* November, 1987 [in Armenian].

[7] During his lifetime, Artemis's father, Garabed, had assets with the French Bank, Credit Lyonnais, in Cairo, Egypt. Beginning in 1939 Artemis sought to claim those assets as Garabed's only heir. To her, an only child and orphan, any inheritance was priceless. Unfortunately, by the mid 1950s, when she focused on the issue, the Egyptian Statute of Limitations of thirty-three years from Garabed's death foreclosed the possibility of Artemis's claim.

[8] In 2000 Artemis related her life story to daughter Muriel which appeared as the 21 page pamphlet, *Story of my Life Artemis Yeramian Mirak* (Weisbaden, Germany, 2000).

[9] John Mirak's letter, probably from 1988, is in Muriel Mirak-Weissbach, *Through the Wall of Fire Armenia—Iraq—Palestine* (Germany, 2009), 28-31. The letter concluded with a wager of $1,000,000 to be donated to McCarthy's chosen charity if John couldn't convince McCarthy of

the existence of the Genocide. For legal reasons, and John's advanced age, the letter was not sent.

[10] Anna Mirakian's memoir, part of a series on the Genocide, and entitled *Verker ou Tsaver* [Wounds and Pains], was published in Antelias, Lebanon, in 1960, and recently translated into English by Dr. Ara Ghazarians, curator of the Armenian Cultural Foundation of Arlington, Massachusetts.

· II ·

# World War One: The Exodus

Zaven's and Artemis's odyssey to the New World, though similar, also require separate narratives.

*Artemis's story:* After leaving her Turkish family for her cousin Joovar's, (whom she also called Ablah), Artemis began her Armenian life. And like many survivors with relatives already in the United States, she, Joovar, Joovar's half sister Siranoush, and nephew Boghos (Paul) made their way to the New World. Joovar's husband, living in Watertown, Massachusetts, was reluctant to feed so many mouths. But his stalwart wife, Joovar, still in Turkey, was adamant: "You either let me bring these orphans with me, or I will not come to you," she wrote to him. "Siranoush is my sister, Boghos is your nephew, and Artemis, my first cousin, they have no one other than me." John Millian relented and they came, a story told in Artemis's words:[1]

*All who had relatives in the U. S.A. were leaving the village. We were all coming to America. This was the sum-*

mer of 1923. We packed our belongings, food and bedding. There was a caravan heading for Aleppo, Syria. Siranoush and I were too young to ride on horseback, so they built two large boxes, like a saddle, and she and I sat in the boxes, ready for the journey. The caravan had four families, all women and children, and the caravan leaders, who were Kurds. This was their livelihood, transporting people from Turkey to Aleppo, Syria.

We would ride all day, then at the end of the day we camped, built campfires, cooked, ate and the spread out our bedding and slept in the fields. Then early at dawn, we would start out again. While riding, all I could see was the sky and the tops of the trees. There were no paved roads, just trails, but the caravan leaders knew where they were taking us.

I don't know how many days or weeks it took us to reach a village. We went through many narrow mountain passes, and crossed many rivers. . . .

One day we were passing a huge eerie mountain. We heard gunshots. There were bandits there, we turned our horses back to the village, afraid to go on. We camped again then at night, we were robbed of our belongings. I remember my Ablah [Joovar] had a satchel, a bag of coins, which she threw to the bandits, saying, "This is all I have, I am a

## II. WORLD WAR ONE: THE EXODUS

*poor woman with three orphans with me." Anyway, they left, after having taken some of our pillows and bedding.*

*The caravan leaders refused to go on, as they were afraid for their lives. They wanted to abandon us. My Ablah, my distant aunt, Margret Dedekian, and another lady, went to see the town officials, asking for help or for some other caravan that could take us to Aleppo. I don't know exactly how much more distance we had to go, but anyway, we had to go on. The next day, the town officials sent six gendarmes to lead us with the caravan. I remember they all wore ammunition, crisscrossing their chests. They looked very official and we felt very secure.*

*Then, at dawn we set out. As we approached the mountain passage, again we heard gunshots, one after another, and another, which just missed our horses. They had planned to rob us, only this time, these six so-called gendarmes were also part of the gang of bandits!*

*By the grace of God, or faith, as you might call it, the bullets that were aimed at us, hit one of the gendarmes, so they started to shoot at one another. At this point, my Ablah. . . gave the order to turn back, turn the caravan, turn the horses and ride hard, and we did, and even to this day I can hear the whizzing of bullets.*

*We came back to where we had started from. We camped in the field all by ourselves, and waited for another caravan to join with. It was a miracle: another caravan came, going to Aleppo, and we joined them. We traveled many many days, weeks, I don't remember exactly.*

*Finally, one morning, we landed in Aintab, then in the city of Aleppo. What a joyous day that was! A safe place, no more camping in the wilderness, no more bandits, or fearing for our lives. Aleppo, as I remember, was a great big city, with lovely pastry shops, and nice clean inns. All of us were together in a large inn, with soft, clean beds, and a courtyard to play in. It was fun for the first time.*

*Upon arrival at the inn, my Ablah told Boghos to take the saddle boxes apart, and break the four corner posts on each box, eight all together. In each post, she had had Boghos pile gold liras, one on top of the other. This is the way she saved all her wealth, gold and more gold, to bring to America. It was enough to fill a large satchel. She was a courageous woman, and had plenty of horse sense. Who would ever think of hiding gold pieces in posts of boxes where the two orphans were travelling?*

*We stayed in Aleppo for three or four months, waiting for our immigration papers. The three orphans, Siranoush, Boghos, . . . and myself, Artemis Yeramian, were to come to America with my Ablah. We were her and her husband John Millian's. . . foster children, and he provided every-*

## II. WORLD WAR ONE: THE EXODUS

*thing for us. I was eight years old, Siranoush was nine, and Boghos was sixteen. Several times we went to the French Consul. At that time Aleppo, Syria was under French government control. We had our pictures taken, papers to be filled out, and finally we left Aleppo and then went to the coast to take a boat to Marseilles.*

*It was terrible, we were packed like cattle at the bottom of the boat, and could not eat the food they served us. It was awful; everyone was seasick, vomiting all over the place.*

*Luckily it was a short trip. We landed in Marseilles, France. We went to an inn, and once again we were comfortable. My. . . Ablah knew some family there and we visited them. Then they took us to some dress shops and my aunt bought us pretty dresses and shoes to come to America. It was a wonderful experience, new clothes, new friends, good French food, and chocolates—it was the first time I had tasted chocolates—delicious!*

*From Marseilles to Paris, we took a train. This, too, was the first time to ride on a train, how wonderful it felt! We landed in Paris, stayed overnight, then went to Le Havre, and boarded a French steamship, the S. S. Suffren French Line. It was in November, perhaps the first or second day of the month. It was cold and rainy, as I looked out of my porthole, but we were happy to the come to U.S. A., a free land, away from all the miseries and the Turkish oppression. America, America, land of freedom!*

*Zaven's story:* After the massacres in Mashgerd, during which the eight- year-old Zaven lost his mother and father, and buried his grandmother and infant brother Yeprad, he lived with a Turkish family probably with his other brother, Vartges. In time he was found by his aunt, Anna Mirakian.

When the war broke out, Anna was also living in Mashgerd with her three children, her husband Garabed having emigrated to the United States in 1912 with the promise to bring her and the children to his new home. The war closed all transportation routes, frustrating her attempts to reach Aleppo with her family. A young mother with ties to the philanthropic Armenian Red Cross, she was repeatedly accused by Turkish authorities of treason, and harboring guns, and searched and beaten, amid offers to save herself by marriage to a Muslim. As the massacres took place in Mashgerd, she counseled her children: "I don't know what is going to happen tomorrow or where we will be staying or where we will end up. No matter what, try not to forget your last name, and the names of your father and mother. The world will change. There will be Armenian survivors,

## II. WORLD WAR ONE: THE EXODUS

who can get your names to your father in America. He will save you."[2]

Soon after, she was sent with her children on a death march to the desert miles from Mashgerd. She was knocked unconscious by a Turkish gendarme, and on waking, found her children had disappeared—never to be found again. She was tormented by their loss, "I had gone mad," she wrote, and contemplated suicide. She returned to Mashgerd, where through harsh field work and menial jobs, she cared for her orphaned nephews, Zaven and Vartges, 'who filled the void of motherhood in my heart."[3] Zaven's reunion with his aunt came after hesitations: "I was afraid to leave the Turkish woman" who had sheltered him, he confessed, for "I had seen the slaughter of the Armenians."[4]

Anna Mirakian recalled their lives and aspirations: *As long as I could earn a piece of dry bread and as long as I could see my brother-in-law's children playing with their make-shift toys forgetting their great sorrows, it was sufficient for me. . . . The life of an orphan had put its. . . mark on their souls. . . . It was a great joy for them when I brought them a piece of sweet or when I boiled grass or some other things and sprayed a pinch of salt on it. . . . Regardless of how much memories of days past tormented us, the hopes of a better future inspired and imbued us with courage. Oh, how I prayed that peace would return, the roads opened, and I could cross the mountains and valleys with my two children and be reunited with my husband.*[5]

The travails of Anna, Zaven, and Vartges took them first to Arabkir, where Near East Relief saved hundreds of Armenian refugees and orphans. Recalled Zaven: "I used to go and get an allowance of wheat for two, and that was enough for a week. The man in charge of Near East Relief was Mr. Knapp. We all thought he was God."[6] After a year in Arabkir, where Anna taught in the National School, she and Zaven, with funds from family in Aleppo, settled there for another year, until they received word and tickets to come to America. On January 25, 1921, she and Zaven were reunited in New York with Garabed Mirakian, Anna's husband and Zaven's uncle. Vartges, who had earlier been placed in an Armenian orphanage in Kharpert, a town near Arabkir, joined the family some time thereafter. For the three, a very long nightmare had ended.

---

[1] Yeramian, 10-12.
[2] Mirakian, 20.
[3] Ibid., 46.
[4] Recollection, Bob Mirak.
[5] Mirakian, 58.
[6] In Mirak-Weissbach, 30.

· III ·

# Settlement and Family: The Beginnings

In the years from their arrival in the United States, Zaven and Artemis settled with their de facto adopted families, attended public schools, got jobs, married (1932) and started a family (1933). Freed from the terrors of genocidal Turkey, they showed great pluck and determination and were happy even as the country plunged into the Great Depression (1929-1939).

On his arrival in the New World in 1921, fourteen-year-old Zaven, his aunt Anna Mirakian, and later his brother Vartges, lived with his uncle, Garabed, in a three decker on Beach Street, in Revere, Massachusetts, a largely immigrant community on the Atlantic Ocean. In the same neighborhood was the Alexander (Tekmejian) family, consisting of widow Lucia and her six children. When Garabed and family moved from Revere, the Mirakian and Alexander families remained close. As years passed, one Alexander worked for Zaven, others became prominent in public life, and all, with unabashed respect, looked to him for advice and guidance.

In Revere Zaven attended the public schools.[1] Moving to Malden with the family, he received a diploma from night school, the immigrants' portal to education; during the day he washed dishes at a downtown Boston hotel. He then enrolled and graduated from the New England Automotive School in Boston. At first he was rebuffed at job seeking: "I went everywhere looking for a job with my diploma and nobody would look at me." But he got a mechanic's job in Boston for $3/week, raised to $6/week, which he recalled "was heaven to me." Joining another garage, which went broke, and unable to find work, he took whatever job was available—as a plumber's apprentice and truck driver—though autos were his first love. In 1928 he returned to car repairs when a fellow Armenian, Jack Berberian, owner of Arlington Dye Works, hired him to repair ADW's trucks, thus beginning Zaven's business and soon residence in the town which was to last until his death seventy-two years later. Ambitious, restless to succeed, in 1932 he joined four other immigrants (three Armenians and a Greek) to form Arlington Center Garage and Service Corporation (to this day the family's flagship entity) to repair autos, sell gas, and buy and sell used cars. Earlier (by 1928 to be specific) Zaven

## III. SETTLEMENT AND FAMILY: THE BEGINNINGS

Mirakian had become John Peter Mirak.[2] For, like other Armenian immigrants who kept their roots but wanted to succeed—the dynamic entrepreneur and philanthropist Stephen Mugardichian became Steve Mugar—there were fewer hills to climb with an Americanized name.

In 1930 or 1931 Artemis Eramian went to work for John Mirak as his bookkeeper. Having arrived in the United States in 1923, she, her cousin Joovar, Siranoush and Paul Millian had lived with Joovar's husband and another immigrant family in East Watertown, Mass., a heavily Armenian district. Soon John Millian built a two-family house on School Street, where Artemis and the family lived until she and Zaven married in 1932.

Like Zaven, Artemis had attended public schools where she demonstrated intellectual abilities but for economic reasons was forced to drop out and work in an Armenian owned clothing factory in Watertown. She retained her ties with a beloved school teacher (Anastasia McMullen) and an abiding interest in literature (more on this later). In the Millian household John and Joovar Millian raised three children of their own. Though she rarely dwelled on it, orphaned Artemis (as well as perhaps Siranoush and Paul) sometimes encountered the pain of being treated like wards and outsiders.

The ties between the two families (Artemis's and Zaven's) dated back to Turkey during World War One. In the chaos of the Genocide, Anna Mirakian had met Joovar Millian. Once resettled close to each other in Greater Boston, they naturally socialized, and as the young and pretty Artemis recalled, she was attracted to Zaven, notwithstanding the attention other males gave her. She particularly remembered that, though Zaven's businesses operated on a shoestring, he always had a fancy car and took the families on weekend picnics.[3]

The two immigrant orphans married in 1932 and lived with John's adoptive family, then in Medford, Mass. A first child, Bob (christened Bedros—for his grandfather—and Haroutiun—"resurrection" in Armenian because he was born on Easter Sunday) was born in 1933. The young couple moved soon after to an unheated three story walkup in Somerville, where Bob's first (makeshift) bed was a bureau drawer. Although Artemis recalled that the bed was comfortable, others attributed Bob's angular personality to this early experience. A second son, Charles Arthur, was born fifteen months later. Within the next six years the family moved from Somerville to a two family home in Arlington, and in 1939 or 1940 to Winchester, which became the family homestead for the next eighteen years.

## III. SETTLEMENT AND FAMILY: THE BEGINNINGS

A third son, Edward Y. Mirak, was born in 1940. (The "Y" was for Yeprad, the infant brother whom Zaven buried during World War One).

Despite the ongoing Great Depression, John Mirak (now known as Johnny) and his Armenian partners forged new businesses. In 1935, the group bought trucks to enter the rental/ leasing business. In the same year, they purchased from the United States Trust Company the garage at 440 Mass. Ave., which housed their businesses. (The price was $50,000—a down payment of $500, a mortgage of $49,425, and monthly payments of $250). The following year they borrowed $7,000 to buy a failed Chevrolet dealership in Arlington and formed Arlington Center Motor Company, the third of their commercial entities (a garage, a dealership, and a trucking company). And they built up a staff of employees.[4]

The ensuing years were tumultuous.[5] Given the number of enterprises, the age of the four partners (in their twenties and thirties), and their personalities—Martin Javian, the first elected president of the dealership, was particularly passionate, disagreements were inevitable; indeed, corporate minutes reflect a stream of resignations, change in positions, and the like. Overriding and exacerbating these was the lack of work, the harsh, grim realities of

5. Zaven, his uncle and aunt, Garabed and Anna Mirakian, and cousin Hovsep, in the United States in 1923. Hovsep is named after a brother who was lost in Turkey during World War One.

6. Artemis in 1926.

7. Wedding photo of John and Artemis, 1932.

8. Artemis with the four children in 1943: from left to right, Bob and Sooky, Eddy in front right, and Muriel in Artemis' lap.

America in deep depression. (Artemis remembered that no job was too trivial for Johnny: calls to their home even in the middle of the night—for a towing job or a wreck—were always welcome.) A climax came in 1939 when the four partners, in deep disagreements, decided to split up. As no one had the cash to buy out the others, Johnny Mirak approached the United States Trust Company, which required him to take out a life insurance policy with the Bank as beneficiary so that in the event of his death, the bank would be reimbursed. With the loan from the bank, he now single-handedly owned three companies: Arlington Center Garage and Service Corporation, Arlington Motor Company (dealership), and Arlington Center Trucking Company. His ambition, intelligence, resourcefulness, and honesty had impressed the bankers, especially one Ira Rachevsky of US Trust.

The breakup of the partnership in 1939 left Johnny Mirak with two important assets. First, his workforce included a handful of capable, experienced mechanics—many of whom stayed as Mirak employees for decades. They were led by Lewis (Lew) Warsky, general manager, and Mary Doherty, office manager, both of whom were highly capable and dedicated employees, then and for years to come. Secondly, the company began its long affiliation with

## III. SETTLEMENT AND FAMILY: THE BEGINNINGS

the New England Telephone and Telegraph Company, by storing and servicing its trucks in the "garage"—the name given to Johnny's businesses. The relationship with NET bore fruit in the following years and decades.

---

[1] Details of his early career are in John Mirak, deposition, April, 1983, in Bob Mirak's personal files.

[2] The official name change was from Zarvin [sic] Peter Mirakian to John Peter Mirak.

[3] Yeramian, *My Life,* 15.

[4] Mirak, deposition.

[5] Records of Arlington Center Garage and Service Corporation and Mirak Chevrolet, 1932-1939.

· IV ·

# The War Years: Alaska, California

The Japanese attack on Pearl Harbor on December 7, 1941 and the American declaration of war the following day severely disrupted domestic life. Military mobilization began immediately, and by February 1942 the war effort found Detroit converted from producing cars and trucks to tanks and airplanes. The Japanese threat to the Pacific West Coast, especially the Alaskan territory and the Aleutian Islands, led the country, also in February 1942, to undertake the construction of the Alaskan (also Alcan) Highway, to protect national interests.[1]

In Boston, Johnny Mirak found himself without product to sell. At the same time, however, he had a trucking company geared to hauling earth for construction projects. Sometime in early 1942 he signed up with the United States government to help build the new Alcan artery. Artemis, with three young children in tow, objected, but to no avail.

Mirak Chevrolet was left under its able managers, Lew Warsky and Mary Doherty.

With two employees (Eddy Modoono and Harold Brown), Johnny took his 18 trucks to the great Northwest (as a subcontractor to David Nassif Company, itself a subcontractor to the Dowell Company.)[2] Their task was to build roads and bridges chiefly at the southern terminus of the highway, in the (Canadian) Yukon Territory. To the north was the Alaska Territory, to the south was British Columbia. The specific locale was near the village of Teslin, bordered by the waters of Nisuthlin Bay and 92-mile-long Teslin Lake.

Johnny Mirak, though articulate with the written word, preferred film as a narrative medium; and his 16 millimeter camera recorded dramatic scenes from 1942-1943. One span shows men clustered in front of the "J. MIRAK ALCAN HIGHWAY GARAGE." Another depicts a bulldozer in the middle of Dead Man Creek accumulating soil, while a backhoe moves earth to construct the Dead Man Creek Bridge. A final section shows Johnny Mirak walking briskly—clearly in his element—supervising construction, moving earth and building—amid towering firs and cavernous lakes.[3]

What was the experience like? Johnny wrote to one relative about the bad roads and described how vehicles

IV. THE WAR YEARS: ALASKA, CALIFORNIA

frequently broke down. As the chief mechanic, he repaired the six-wheel dump trucks, sometimes in his garage, but often out on the tundra. When temperatures went to -30° degrees Fahrenheit, fires were built under the trucks to start or repair them. And road conditions were tough. One observer described spring conditions: "The ground was so soft that one truck could not follow in another's tracks without bogging down. . . . Sometimes you would see a D-8 [bulldozer] hauling a 'train' of three or four trucks, dragging them through the gumbo. Our one and a half ton dumps were too light for this going and many springs and axles were broke [sic]."[4]

The long summer days and short nights let the men play baseball until near midnight. Johnny, who enjoyed hunting, bought contraband ammunition from local Indians in exchange for cigarettes. There was humor as well. One Mirak employee (Harold Brown) was told that brass filings in a local river were actually gold ore. Brown dug out large quantities and mailed them home to his wife. A local jeweler soon informed her of their real (negligible) value.[5]

More soberly, the winters were brutal. January 1943, when Johnny Mirak was there, "was a month of bitter cold. Broken-down equipment began to accumulate in the repair shops. . . . It was often so cold (-71° F was the record low that month near the Alaskan border; -60° F in the Fort Nelson area) that all outside work stopped. On such days, the best place to be was next to a roaring stove, but even that could be dangerous."[6] Lodgings were in makeshift wooden cabins, liquor was rationed and very expensive, and poker games—where money was abundant and goods were not—often yielded fabulous pots. But the remoteness, isolation, and absence of families took their toll. Johnny remembered that many men were broken by the experience. (Contracts were commonly for six to nine months, but employee Eddy Modoono lasted only nine weeks). Johnny returned home twice during his fifteen-month-tour in Alaska.

By mid 1943 work on the Alcan Highway was slowing; by August, the project was nearly completed. Eager to keep his fleet of trucks working, Johnny turned to GMAC (the General Motors Acceptance Corporation, the financing arm of General Motors) for help in placing his vehicles. California, with its armament industry, was the answer. So, with an agreement with the Public Roads Administration of the Federal Works Agency, Johnny shipped the trucks to Long Beach, and eventually to the federal Naval Air Weapons Station at China Lake. Before traveling to California, Johnny returned home in mid-1943 to an exuberant family which

## IV. THE WAR YEARS: ALASKA, CALIFORNIA

then learned, with dismay and sadness, that yet another lengthy separation was in the works. Artemis, now with a fourth child—Muriel—was crestfallen.[7]

If a land route to Alaska was needed in 1942 to protect against Japanese attacks, by 1943 the allied military required facilities to build and test its latest weapons: rockets. The Naval Air Weapons Station at China Lake, some 150 miles northeast of Los Angeles, on the western end edge of the Mojave Desert was chosen—for its "near-perfect flying weather year-round and practically unlimited visibility." Proximity to the scientists at CalTech was also crucial. The entire facility encompassed 1.1 million acres—mostly uninhabited. Its outpost was the hamlet of Inyokern, which supported a population of 55 in 1940.[8]

Johnny Mirak's eighteen six-wheelers became a cog in the gigantic construction effort at China Lake. In striking contrast to Alaska, daytime temperatures ran above 100 degrees; at night they fell to 50 degrees. Sand and heat produced major mechanical problems. And the endless succession of cloudless days created monotony. But it was paying work and vital to the war effort, producing then and to this day the military's most lethal weaponry.

Bob remembers regular letters to the family originating from the Don Hotel in Inyokern. A photo of Johnny Mirak, then aged thirty-seven or thirty-eight, depicts him barechested, deeply tanned, with a pith helmet and boots—a Tarzan-like image. Again, a builder in his element. Always mindful of development potential, when he and some friends vacationed to then nascent Las Vegas, he suggested that the group buy land in this boom time, a thought that was quickly (and foolishly) dismissed. Time passed, and with a two-year tour of duty under his belt, and the end of the war in the Pacific, Johnny sold his fleet of trucks in California and returned home, an event greeted with joy and relief by all.

---

[1] Heath Twitchell, *Northwest Epic The Building of the Alaska Highway* (New York, 1992), is the standard account. There are useful maps in the Wikipedia entry on the "Alaska Highway."

[2] The contractors involved awarded Johnny Mirak certificates of recognition.

[3] Films by Johnny Mirak, in personal possession of Bob Mirak.

[4] Twitchell, 209.

[5] Interview, Ed Mirak, Sept. 19, 2011.

[6] Twitchell, 248.

[7] Although Muriel was the family's fourth child, Johnny Mirak wanted more. But Artemis refused. It was one of the few contests Johnny ever lost.

[8] Internet, California State Military Department, Historic California Posts, Naval Air Weapons Station, China Lake, is the source here.

· Ⅴ ·

# The Early Postwar Years: Halcyon Days

With World War Two over and Johnny Mirak back home, he eagerly expanded his automotive businesses, capitalizing on his intelligence and restless energy, as well as a booming US economy. His real estate projects also date from this period. At the same time, at his initiative, the family established its summer home in the Rangeley Lakes of Maine, which for the next half century and more provided wonderful times of relaxation and sports for all. Also, the second generation was taking its first steps toward maturity and college educations. It was a time of optimism, unsullied by sickness or heartbreak.

Soon after hostilities ended in June 1945, Detroit started churning out its cars and trucks to consumers starved for new vehicles; and Chevrolet, General Motors' leading product and America's best seller, brought handsome rewards. Mirak Chevrolet, Inc. (the new name from December, 1945, of the Arlington Center Motor Company) became prominent and profitable, though without bloated payoffs. (Many dealers accepted "under- the-table" cash for hard to get cars; John Mirak balked at the practice, hewing to his motto that "an ounce of honesty is worth a pound of cleverness.") Tucked off Massachusetts Avenue with no street visibility, his dealership needed street frontage; by 1948, Mirak Chevrolet had purchased an abutting Massachusetts Avenue furniture store and converted it into a first-class office building and showroom, with ground-to-ceiling glass fronts. (Lew Warsky, Mirak's trusted general manager, deemed the glass fronts unnecessary, to which Johnny Mirak replied, "Lew, you could limit viewing to peepholes in solid walls; but we need a statement!"). Two three-story apartment buildings abutting the showroom were purchased in 1953 and moved 150 feet back from the street—by a construction company from Oklahoma—to make way for a much needed used car lot, thus making another Mirak Chevrolet statement.

With business booming, local Chevrolet dealers organized the Massachusetts Chevrolet Dealers Association to attain advertising clout. In 1948 Johnny Mirak was elected its first president. (Later he attained the same post with the New England Chevrolet Dealers Association.) Though his English needed honing, his intellect and personality were

## V. THE EARLY POSTWAR YEARS: HALCYON DAYS

first class. As the Association's spokesman, he appeared on Red Sox television broadcasts, sponsored in part by the dealers. In the process he got to know Ted Williams and other sports celebrities who became lifelong friends. It was some move from the immigrant days in Revere and Malden.

As the auto business expanded, in 1947 Johnny Mirak ventured into real estate, first building a 25,000 square foot garage in East Arlington for the trucks of the New England Telephone Company, which had earlier been housed in the Arlington Center garage. Amassing the various real estate parcels and obtaining proper zoning for the 102,000 square foot lot weren't easy. (One truculent, probably anti-immigrant, neighbor told Johnny that "if Mirak is for it, I am against it.") But dogged determination and the backing of trusted tenants, (notably NET) yielded a handsome yellow brick structure. A second floor of 25,000 first-class office space, also for NET, was added some time later. (Johnny called the original real estate entity "Yukon Realty Trust.")

An accomplished businessman, Johnny Mirak also loved outdoor sports, especially hunting and fishing. His children still remember the buck with antlers or the doe lashed to the fender of his Chevy, the fruits of a November outing he would bring home to Winchester. In late 1945, or perhaps before, he also discovered the Rangeley Lakes, in northwest Maine, and especially its great trout and landlocked salmon fishing. In 1946 the family, with friends, spent two weeks in a cabin on Lake Mooselookmeguntic. The year after, while Artemis and the four children vacated on Cape Cod, Johnny Mirak surprised the family by purchasing an estate on Lake Mooselookmeguntic, which he aptly dubbed Yukon Lodge. (Eight years earlier he had purchased the home in Winchester without any prior notice or consultation with the family).

Yukon Lodge, the family's summer residence until John's death in 2000, and now owned by son Edward, contained a three-bedroom main house, a four-bedroom guest house, a caretaker's cabin, two garages, a boat house, and smaller sheds. To maintain the premises, the family hired a cook, caretaker, and waitress.

To some, Yukon Lodge was an expensive luxury; to Johnny Mirak, it was a family home where he taught the boys how to fish and hunt. Indeed, some of his happiest days were spent on a boat with his family and his dog, as he sang songs from the Old Country. However, Yukon Lodge was also a critical business investment. For, from its beginnings in 1947, he and Artemis and the kids hosted scores of John's business associates, contacts, and friends, many of whom were vital to further his enterprises.

9. John Mirak during World War Two on the Alaska/Canada (Alcan) Highway.

10. John Mirak at the Red Rock Canyon, Mojave Desert, California, December 24, 1944.

11. John Mirak with long-time trusted Mirak Chevrolet general manager, Lewis (Lew) Warsky.

12. Newly opened showroom of Mirak Chevrolet, 1952.

13. Artemis with fellow Armenian American women, probably the Armenian Women's School Union of Arlington, Mass., which supported a Saturday Armenian school for the second generation. Artemis also belonged to a social group, the "Jolly Eight," but this photo is of nine women.

14. Yukon Lodge, Oquossoc/Rangeley, Maine, the family's summer home from 1947.

15. Vartges Mirakian, John's surviving younger brother, in military uniform.

Who were these guests? The very first year, all the local Chevrolet dealers were invited. In that period Metropolitan Chevrolet was run by a zone manager; and he and his family spent from two weeks to a month annually, as guests. Chevrolet district managers and even executives from Detroit were feted—as were executives from New England Telephone. In the 1960s, John Collins, then Mayor of Boston, spent weeks with Mary Collins and their children at Yukon Lodge. Sports figures like Bump Hadley of the Red Sox, and Frank Egan of the Boston Bruins were also welcomed. And on and on.

To the economic motive were added obligations to family. Often sandwiched in between personalities were relatives—cousins, aunts and uncles, close immigrant friends. And with great generosity, the friends of the second generation were welcomed, fed, and feted. It was an extraordinary outpouring of hospitality, laced with business and family overtones.

But the entertaining was not without its emotional costs, especially on Artemis as hostess. Anxious to support and assist her husband, and a vital core of the successful enterprise, she cheerfully assumed multiple roles. These included supervising meals, instructing the help as it cleaned the buildings and grounds, helping entertain the

## V. THE EARLY POSTWAR YEARS: HALCYON DAYS

guests (and occasionally smoothing over inevitable tensions), all the while supervising four children, and their friends, especially while her husband was away in Boston on business. These were no easy tasks. Indeed, they were giant responsibilities, and they took their toll, fatiguing Artemis and probably contributing to problems soon to confront her.

To these tensions the younger generation was oblivious. For them Yukon Lodge meant relaxation for Bob (golf) and Sooky (fishing and hunting). As late teenagers, they also partied at local "joints." Eddy, at an early age, became an accomplished fly fisherman at a stream in nearby Oquossoc, to the envy of older men casting fishing lines nearby. And sister Muriel became a stable hand and rode horses at nearby P. K. Ellis's farm. For the family the times were idyllic.[1]

---

[1] Information from personal memory of Bob Mirak.

## · VI ·

# Tragedy and Trauma

Tragedy struck the family in the winter of 1953, some five years after the purchase of the summer home in Maine. Its traumatic effects were both immediate and lengthy, running like a red skein through the family's subsequent history.

At the time Bob was a sophomore at Williams and Sooky a freshman at Colgate, where he found studies no challenge and had plenty of time for hunting grouse and partridge. In late January, at home on vacation, Sooky took a girlfriend on the newly completed Route 128 super highway—for a driving lesson. With her at the wheel, and Sooky in the passenger seat, they tried to negotiate an off ramp. Whether the ramp was under construction or there was sand on the road is uncertain but the car flipped over, and Sooky smashed his neck against the door pillar. There were no seatbelts; the girl was unscathed; but Sooky sustained major injuries to his spinal chord. Although no one knew or dreamed it to be possible, the accident would make him a quadriplegic until his death fifty-three years later. It also irrevocably scarred the family.

Sooky's first care was at nearby Lynn Hospital. Spinal chord treatments were in their infancy. To stabilize his condition after surgery—and this seems gruesome—he was put into traction: a metal screw attached to a stiff rod was drilled into his skull; and this was tied to the headboard. No direct intake of fluids was permitted. And this regimen continued at Lynn Hospital for weeks and weeks.

Bob first heard of the accident by phone in Williamstown; and Anna Mirakian, helping at the Winchester home, assured him that all would be well. John and Artemis, who rushed to the hospital, were joined by family physician Edward Levenson. John, though hardened by massacre and exile, could not contain his tears.[1] Eddy Modoono, one of John's faithful employees dating to the Alaskan highway, was given the thankless task of towing and disposing of the wrecked coupe.

After a lengthy hospital stay, Sooky returned to the Winchester home little improved; the formal dining room on the first floor became his bedroom until the family moved some years later to Arlington. Nurses, like one Miss Dionne, became critical, much appreciated fixtures in the household.

## VI. TRAGEDY AND TRAUMA

His grave condition brought many close friends and well-intentioned amateurs with suggestions for bizarre remedies. Even by the summer of 1953 Sooky was in no condition to travel, so Yukon Lodge remained mostly unoccupied. In time, however, he graduated to a wheelchair. Studious and bright, he then fortunately enrolled in the home-study program of the Division of General Education at Boston University, in which full-time faculty came weekly as instructors and tutors to the family home at 131 Cambridge Street, Winchester. This led in two years to an Associate Degree. With the very generous help of family friend Harry Adamian who drove him to the main campus of Boston University, in 1958 he graduated with a BA in Business Administration. Clearly education was a godsend to him.

Dislocating the family's living quarters, the accident led John to seek a home equipped with wheelchair access. A large lot at the high point of Morningside Drive, in Arlington, was selected; and a spacious single story, modern home was built, especially adapted for wheelchair use. The move to the neighboring community forced Eddy and Muriel to transfer from Winchester High School to Arlington High School, disrupting their social ties. The move also reflected the family's dawning realization that, after five years of recuperation, Sooky was destined to be a life-long cripple.

GENOCIDE SURVIVORS, COMMUNITY BUILDERS...

Unnoticed by most, the illness gravely affected Artemis, who as a mother at home not only cared for her second son but also on a daily basis painfully saw the possibility of his recovery slip by. Probably exhausted as well by her responsibilities in caring for the family, and those in the summers at Yukon Lodge, she was unable to cope with the trauma of the accident. As a result, she escaped into an understandable refuge of emotional despair: in 1955 she had her first mental breakdown which erupted in an episode characterized by a sense of worthlessness. Muriel recalled her screaming in the middle of the night, "Throw me in the garbage can. I am no good."[2] Hospitalized in nearly Concord, she underwent shock treatments, then standard but now regarded as near barbaric. After a protracted stay, she returned home, dazed, her recent memories (and depression) obliterated. Some time later, a freak accident—falling partially under a family automobile at the family's home—triggered the second emotional retreat and further shock therapy. (Friends ruefully noted how the automobile, which brought the family success, involved tragic consequences as well.) Sooky's condition, she later stated, was her "cross to bear."

Hard times extended beyond the immediate family to John's younger brother, Vartges. As newly arrived immigrants, the brothers had lived in Revere, with Aunt

## VI. TRAGEDY AND TRAUMA

Anna Mirakian's family. In the early 1930s, when John and Artemis married and set up their own household Medford, Vartges moved in with them. During World War Two he entered the United States Army. A handsome photo of Vartges in uniform testifies to his military tour of duty. With peacetime, he worked for his older brother at the "garage," and then opened up a gas station nearby in Arlington. He soon married and in time he and his wife, Ann Berejikian, had two sons. But like Job, Vartges was beset by troubles: his business failed, he and his wife divorced. Sometime in the late 1950s he moved to Chicago, where he worked at the Midwest Hotel as its maintenance superintendent for some years. He then contracted bladder cancer and died not long after.

Just before his death, John Mirak called Bob into his office, told him that Vartges was in Chicago, dying, and that he, Bob, should go to Chicago to arrange for Vartges's funeral and last rites—this because John and Artemis were scheduled for a Chevrolet trip to Mexico. Bob was further instructed NOT to tell Vartges's ex-wife or sons about his illness and funeral plans. Bob subsequently ruefully regretted following his father's instructions (surely as Vartges's brother, John, should have gone to Chicago, and surely Vartges's family should have been included in the situation)—and for years Bob believed he had dutifully complied with his father's orders. And later he apologized to Vartges's son Alan for his actions. (Ironically, in 2011, as he began this memoir and spoke to Alan about it, Bob learned that in fact he HAD told Alan and his brother about their father's illness and that both had traveled to Chicago in time for a final farewell. That piece of information helped a great deal.)

What created the rupture between John and Vartges? According to Artemis, Vartges "drank a lot" and his wife Ann was "headstrong."[3] It is clear that John expended considerable energy and resources to help Vartges in his business venture and establishing a family; but it was also probably true that Vartges found it very difficult to live under John's shadow, as a younger, less resilient, less independent sibling.

Together, Vartges's death, Artemis's illnesses and Sooky's catastrophic accident produced a mountain of trials. Life was taking a heavy toll.

---

[1] Ed Mirak recalled that the accident and ensuing paralysis were "devastating to Mother and Dad, who after the war were just beginning to enjoy life and prosperity." Interview, Sept. 19, 2011.

[2] Interview, Muriel Mirak-Weissbach, September 29, 2011.

[3] Yeramian, 19.

## · VII ·

# Revival and Growth

In the midst of the family's trials, the family's leader, John Mirak, never faltered. A survivor of massacres and exile, as well as the struggles of life in a new land, he persevered. For him, if life presented financial opportunities, it also entailed challenges which he relished; echoing sentiments as old as Plutarch, he remarked, "I would rather live one day as a lion than a thousand years as a lamb."

An early task, after building a "wheelchair friendly" home for Sooky, was to find him a meaningful job. With his business degree, Sooky soon became indispensable at Mirak Chevrolet as John's "nuts and bolts" financial and personnel manager. After some time working out of the "old garage," Sooky had an office of his own in the main office/showroom building. Yukon Lodge was similarly made "wheelchair friendly," with ramps, bedroom, and bathing facilities. And John took great pleasure and pride in outfitting boats and lifts to enable Sooky to enjoy his cherished fishing pastime. At Yukon Lodge, entertainment of friends, relatives, and business associates continued though at a slower pace. And for once, a near tragedy ended well: in the summer of 1955, the family speedboat with Muriel, Artemis and John aboard, hit submerged rocks, sank quickly and forced the three to make their way in the Maine darkness to land and eventual rescue. A harrowing episode turned out well. Perhaps fortune was beginning to smile on the family.

At the same time that John and Artemis resumed life in Rangeley, John's mind and heart were also fixed on building--businesses and structures. His children later observed that he was fundamentally a Roman—a builder and engineer. One example stands out. Sometime in the 1970s, Bob, his wife Alice, and John traveled to Las Vegas for an automobile convention. During their stay the three visited the Hoover Dam on the Colorado River and in time took the elevator to the base. Looking up at the massive 725 foot vertical expanse of concrete, it was clear what John was thinking: "that's something I would have liked to have built."

As noted earlier, his first construction venture was the 25,000 square foot garage for New England Telephone. This led to a second floor of equal size (in 1968). By this time

## VII. REVIVAL AND GROWTH

two other projects had been completed. In 1962, relying on his connections with NET, he purchased a one-story, 12,500 square foot Atlantic and Pacific (A&P) supermarket and converted it into a two-story, 25,000 square foot NET office building. Then there was "Mattapan," a project in a transitional section of the city of Boston. Painfully amassing parcels through purchase and auction, he partnered with an Armenian American engineer/ businessman and, with Bob's help, built a 208 unit, four building, four story apartment complex called Morton Village. This was through the Federal Housing Administration. An impressive undertaking (one of the largest in the city of Boston), Morton Village provided affordable quality housing to Boston's families. Then in the 1970s, he purchased two large garages occupied by the New England Telephone Company.

But John Mirak remained faithful to his first love, automobiles, and his quest to make Mirak Chevrolet an exemplary center of service and consequently a pillar of financial strength. One source of revenue was a fleet of leased vehicles, which would yield profits and supply vehicles for resale. Hence, Mirak Leasing. Similarly, in 1977, the company purchased a Thrifty RentACar franchise.[1] Located at Boston's Logan Airport, in Arlington, and four other locales, it served Mirak's growing customer base. The company was becoming an institution, and its founder was accordingly recognized by the prestigious Ben Franklin Quality Dealer Award in 1967 (and later, in 1986). Mindful also of the younger generation's aspirations, in 1974 he purchased a Chevrolet dealership in Winthrop, Mass. for son Eddy; it became Ed Mirak Chevrolet.

By the late 1970s, Mirak Chevrolet, with its 100-plus employees, was situated in four separate locations in Arlington; and a new town zoning bylaw deemed its hub in Arlington Center non-conforming. This meant that, if a fire destroyed the buildings, they could not be rebuilt. Although some family members opposed the idea, John Mirak, now in his seventies, embarked on his most ambitious project to date: to relocate and consolidate the dealership in Arlington Heights, some four miles to the northwest. With Sooky now the dealership principal of Mirak Chevrolet and son Bob in the real estate side of the business, having left a teaching post at Boston University, he began amassing a real estate holding totaling over six acres, or about 277,000 square feet.

To obtain approvals, the project required
—18 public hearings including Arlington Town Meeting

## VII. REVIVAL AND GROWTH

— creative financing, since the prime lending rate was near 20 per cent

— renovation of an existing 32,000 square foot garage; construction of a 30,000 square foot service department and a 16,000 square foot two story state-of-the-art showroom.

Johnny Mirak's vision was that the new location would be the cornerstone for a family enterprise reaching into the distant future. Thus, when his architects proposed a metal ("Butler") building for the new service department and told him that such a building would last forty years, John Mirak vetoed the proposal in favor of a brick and block building that would last for eighty years!

The new Mirak Chevrolet became Johnny Mirak's pride and joy. At its official opening on June 1, 1984, General Motors dignitaries and local officials were joined by the United States Speaker of the House Thomas P. "Tip" O'Neill, Jr., who spoke of his friend John Mirak's contributions to business and society. Thereafter, Chevrolet officials regularly inspected the complex to admire its state-of-the-art delivery systems. And daily, John Mirak visited each department to check on developments and commend his first-rate workforce. At age 77 Johnny Mirak could rightly be proud of his business accomplishments.

But business dynamics required more. By the mid 1980s, European and especially Asian imports were making major inroads with American consumers. Although the family's loyalties, especially John's, Charlie's and Ed's, were with Detroit and especially General Motors, in 1985 the family purchased a Lincoln-Mercury, Nissan franchise. Then, in 1992, the family added a Hyundai franchise and two years later erected a first-class Hyundai showroom to complement its Chevrolet counterpart. In the language of the industry, the company had become a large multi-point dealership.

*John Mirak as entrepreneur* One day, in the 1960s, a portly New England Telephone Company employee had an exchange with Johnny Mirak and called him "Lucky." Johnny responded by pointing to his trim physique and saying, "It was hard work, my friend, not luck." Indeed, especially in the early days, Johnny Mirak had worked 20 hour days, and was often carried home exhausted. But what explained his success was far more than hard work. For one thing, as one lead attorney said, "He was smart, very smart." Seated in his favorite chair at home, or in the office, he was usually deep in thought, pondering a next move, a "what if," or "suppose that." Thoughtful, he was always far reaching in his plans. And he loved the art of a

## VII. REVIVAL AND GROWTH

deal. To be sure, he was not always successful. A greenhorn in the 1920s, he bought waterfront land which at low tide was valuable, but which disappeared at high tide. And no real estate project, beginning with the Telephone Company garage in 1957, was ever easy. But time and again he produced fertile solutions to make the project work. Clearly, he had relied on trusted co-workers. From the late 1930s, Lew Warsky and Mary Doherty shepherded the companies. Son Sooky worked at the dealership and eventually became its invaluable dealer principal; he also ran the leasing and rental companies. Ed Mirak was Sooky's right hand man; and Bob helped with the real estate.

Relying on experienced help, John Mirak also nurtured ties with financial institutions, beginning with the United States Trust Company, and then with local banks (Harvard Trust and Arlington National Bank) which assisted him as he served usefully on their governing boards. His relations with New England Telephone were critical to his success; and he similarly fostered bonds with Chevrolet Motor Division. His dealings with political figures and statesmen should not be overlooked. And in all of these ties, he was resourceful, persuasive, straightforward, and honorable. The fact that he was socially gregarious, great fun to be with, and a true sportsman were additional assets. He was a presence without question.

His focus on real estate deserves one additional consideration. Once Mirak Chevrolet was established after World War Two, he spent much of his career in developing land and buildings. To explain his focus, he frequently said, "God only made so much land." But it may also be that, as an orphan exiled from his homeland, he found in land and what he could put on it, a re-creation of what history had deprived him of; that is, land and buildings gave him roots in a world distant from his ancestral home. No one ever asked him about this, and how much of it he understood in these terms is hard to determine; but it is worth reflecting on to understand what motivated his decision making in his business life.

---

[1] The Thrifty RentACar franchise operated as Mirak RentACar. Other sources chiefly from personal memory of Bob Mirak

· VIII ·

# John Mirak, Community and Philanthropy

What is astonishing is that, while building his companies and helping Artemis raise a family, Johnny Mirak made such a full-fledged commitment to philanthropy and community. Funding local, national, and international (especially Armenian) causes, participating in civic boards and charities, and above all subsidizing and leading a distinguished private library and museum—the Armenian Cultural Foundation—he simultaneously engaged his energies and intellect to the benefit of all. At the same time contributions to local and national political figures provided access to and friendship with those with influence.

The wellsprings of the charitable giving came most directly from a religious conviction—that if his life, and that of his brother, Vartges, had been spared, and that he particularly had been blessed with success, it was for some reason. Why otherwise had they been saved and why had he "made it" in a foreign land? From gratitude, wonder, and probably survivor guilt, he felt compelled to repay society through donations and service. At the same time, he clearly understood the dynamics of American political society.

His earliest continuous service was to Arlington's Symmes Hospital, whose board saw in Johnny Mirak a "can-do" individual. For three decades he served on its board, its executive and building committees, and chaired fund-raising campaigns. The hospital expanded during his term, where his attendance record at meetings was "unbeatable," and he took special pride in the emergency room, where a plaque displayed his words, "We will care for you and comfort you," surely an echo of his orphan days. Prosaic as it may seem, he reveled at its visitor-friendly, newly asphalted parking lot, recalling the Alaskan Highway experience.

Not a regular reader, except for the Bible, he was approached by the Town's Robbins Library board and generously donated to its handsomely refurbished Reading Room as a place of study and reflection. In 1989, after he acquired parcels for the new Mirak Chevrolet, he donated to the Town the historically important Jefferson Cutter House (1817), then located on the dealership property. No Arlington charity—from the Boys Club, to the Association for Retarded Citizens, to the newly formed Little League—

## VIII. JOHN MIRAK, COMMUNITY AND PHILANTHROPY

was without John Mirak's helping hand. Quite sincerely, he wanted to repay the Town for helping him succeed.

On a state-wide level he served from 1958 to 1962 on Massachusetts Governor Foster Furcolo's Board of Educational Assistance and locally for years on Arlington's Redevelopment Board. Arlington's Banks—Harvard Trust and Arlington National Bank—profited from his advice and business, although he resigned from the latter when its officers hired relatives he deemed unqualified for their posts.

Johnny Mirak also understood that money talks. A lifelong Democrat—a great Roosevelt supporter (like most immigrants)—he faithfully donated to political campaigns on the local, state, and federal level often delegating son Bob, then in graduate school, to attend functions for Senator Ted Kennedy, Speaker Tip O'Neill, Jr., (whose library at Boston College also received donations), Representative Joseph Kennedy, and a host of others. A solicitation from the politically connected Roman Catholic Archdiocese was rarely overlooked. Boston's Mayor John Collins and family also shared in his largesse. Johnny Mirak liked and admired these men for their service, and at the same time enjoyed the attention his donations bestowed.

Johnny Mirak never forgot his Armenian roots. No reputable charity was overlooked. Prominent was the family's parish, St. James Armenian Apostolic Church, in Watertown, but Catholic and Protestant Armenian churches also received funds. An important beneficiary, for obvious emotional reasons, was the Armenian Tubercular Sanatorium, in Antelias, Lebanon. He also became a benefactor of the Armenian General Benevolent Union, the Armenians' oldest (1906) charity of its type. The National Association for Armenian Studies and Research (NAASR) and the Armenian Assembly benefitted as well. In 1978 he was awarded the prestigious (Armenian) Ellis Island Award, and received many other commendations from Armenian organizations.

Of all his charitable causes, the dearest to his heart, the one most costly to him financially and emotionally, was the Armenian Cultural Foundation—a distinguished library and museum. Not very well read but aware, as the gifted and highly intelligent man that he was, that the written word and historical record were important to culture, he took up the responsibility for establishing the Foundation in Arlington and directing and single-handedly financing it for over 30 years.

The Armenian Cultural Foundation was incorporated in Boston in 1945 by Vahan Topalian, an Armenian immigrant, tailor by trade but bibliophile by profession. Its mission was "to establish and maintain. . .a library and to

16. 30 Mystic Street, Arlington. Originally a one-story Atlantic and Pacific (A&P) supermarket which John purchased in 1962, and added a second floor for the New England Telephone and Telegraph Company (NET). Building currently houses a division of the Massachusetts Department of Children and Families.

17. The showroom of the "new" Mirak Chevrolet, opened in 1984.

18. Mirak Chevrolet's new Service Center.

19. Side view of the new Service Center.

20. John Mirak with Set Momjian, one-time US. Ambassador to the United Nations, at Ellis Island, September 23, 1978. Both were recipients of the Ellis Island Award for distinguished community service.

21. Jefferson Cutter House, built in 1817 and donated by the Mirak Family to the Town of Arlington in 1989. Now situated in the heart of Arlington Center, the JCH is a focus of community activities and was placed on the National Register in 1992.

22. The Armenian Cultural Foundation, Arlington, Mass.

## VIII. JOHN MIRAK, COMMUNITY AND PHILANTHROPY

hold literary meetings to disseminate knowledge. . .of a literary nature for the advancement of culture in general and Armenian culture in particular."[1] Housed in a handsome five-story brownstone on Boston's Beacon Hill and run for a decade by Topalian and a board of elderly trustees, in 1961 it was to be taken by eminent domain by the Boston Redevelopment Authority for a state office building. In distress Topalian turned for help to John Mirak, a donor with a good community reputation. Mirak, offered the post of president of the Foundation, declined it, citing family and business burdens, only to learn soon after that the Foundation's trustees had elected him president of the Foundation and that he had to appear in court on the land taking case. Characteristically, he rolled up his sleeves and went to work as he

— attended the lengthy court sessions, which yielded a decent settlement for the Foundation;

— provided Topalian with an apartment at no expense, the first of many such kindnesses over the years;

— after a lengthy search found a new home for the Foundation in a Victorian mansion in Arlington;

— added the Great Hall, a 2,200 square foot front room with 14-foot ceilings to showcase the Foundation's magnificent Armenian collections, scores of priceless first editions in the major Western languages, and magnificent objets d'art.

— single handedly financed the institution through his John Mirak Foundation, established in 1971.

Topalian also became a guest every Sunday at John and Artemis's home in Arlington. He also had unlimited support from Mirak employees for transportation, shopping, and laundry. Clearly, John Mirak had adopted the older gentleman as his surrogate father, in an attempt to replace the paternal relationship of which history had deprived him. In addition John had extraordinary respect for Topalian's learning, something which he also had been deprived of.

And the Foundation, with Topalian as curator and Mirak as board president and benefactor, continued on a quiet course until the late 1970s, when Topalian, advancing in age and suffering dementia, was exploited first by an Armenian housekeeping couple, then by the head priest of the Armenian Catholic Church in Cambridge, Mass., to give away the Foundation and its priceless contents to the religious order. However, it was the Foundation's Board and not Topalian who owned the properties. A protracted, expensive legal battle ensued. Artemis feared that the

## VIII. JOHN MIRAK, COMMUNITY AND PHILANTHROPY

anxiety it bred would kill her husband. Happily, a court declared in the Foundation's favor, though the episode cost John Mirak much grief as well as his treasured relationship with the older gentleman. Topalian died in 1983, and in the late 1990s John Mirak turned over his prized jewel to gifted community individuals led by the family's younger generation now coming to maturity.[2]

---

[1] Armenian Cultural Foundation, Articles of Organization, November, 1945.

[2] A brief account of the history of the Armenian Cultural Foundation is in Robert Mirak, "Crises in the Institution: The Armenian Cultural Foundation," *The Armenians of New England* (Belmont, MA., 2004).

## · IX ·

# Growing Up a Mirak

The Great Depression (1929–1939) shaped the children's earliest recollections. Bob's first memory (1937 or 1938) was a Works Project Administration (WPA) crew digging up his street, in Arlington. And he remembered that money, then so scarce, and no matter how little, was precious. In the two decker on Dartmouth Street, Arlington, the Miraks, on the second floor, had the only telephone. Neighbors who used the phone left a valuable nickel after every call. To save money, Artemis bottled fruits and vegetables while Bob and Sooky harvested *perper* (a green leaf) in a neighboring field for salads. During the war years and rationing, Artemis also collected cans of fat needed for the war effort—to make explosives. And Bob and Sooky got to see Red Sox baseball games only after redeeming these cans of fat for cash at a local grocery. Money during the Depression and later was never trumpeted as important and large bills were not to be shown. Hard times brought powerful lessons.

But if the Great Depression formed early values, it was naturally the presence of Artemis and John that most influenced personality and behavior. To be sure, there were many Johns: the early parent, the one away from home during the War, the ambitious and successful entrepreneur, the more relaxed grandfather in his 70s and 80s, and the stroke-ridden patriarch after age 90. But the most formative experiences came from the early years of a driven, highly disciplined, and demanding father who had survived much and expected much.

Two examples. In 1938 or 1939, Sooky (age four or five) was caught playing with matches under the porch at 16 Dartmouth Street. Instead of discipline on the spot, John drove him to the Arlington Police Station, told the officer on duty of the offence, and suggested that Sooky be locked up there and then. Terrified, Sooky promised good behavior and returned home with a lesson he never forgot. He never lit matches again as a youngster. In 1951 Bob entered Williams College with a distinguished public high school record but with no savvy about prep school dress and talk so current at the College. After the first week of rushing fraternities, he was turned down—deemed unworthy—at all eleven fraternities. At home the next week salving his rejection and humiliation, his mother suggested that she

## IX. GROWING UP A MIRAK

complain to the dean of the college. But John said flatly, "It's the best thing that could happen to him." The experience would toughen up Bob; and that was that; no consolation there. (It should be pointed out that Bob joined a fraternity in his sophomore year.)

In between there were few compromises. If any of the children offered the explanation "I thought" to justify an error, John would reply, "Don't think, know." Accomplishment in school wasn't applauded but expected. Bob, Sooky and Muriel passed those tests but Eddy, though talented, had other interests. Nor did John directly praise high achievement. Rather, as Bob recalls, the words "job well done" came from second-hand sources like John's business associates. Compliments never came directly from John, though they were very much appreciated.

A psychiatrist once remarked that John was very critical in order to protect himself from rivals. However, it is more likely that the immigrant generation—especially males—did not offer direct praise—as well as affection—because such was frowned on in the Old Country. Of course, John's edges softened as he grew older, achieved financial success, and greeted grandchildren.

Artemis was much more compassionate. To be sure, during the War years, she was overwhelmed: John was away, she had four children in tow, and no role models to depend on. Still, she cushioned life with sympathy and attention, not only by "giving in" to the youthful requests of the children, but more importantly in touching ways by listening and reading to them. And this was expressed in copious readings from Mark Twain's *Huckleberry Finn,* Shakespeare's *Merchant of Venice,* and other masterpieces. For that they were all grateful.

And she was full of encouragement. In 1955, Bob received a scholarship from Williams to attend Oxford University for two years, at a time when Sooky was confined to a wheelchair, living at home and needing company. Yet Artemis wrote the following striking note to Bob:

*Last night when you called and gave me the good news. . .I didn't know what to say. My only thought was that you will be away from home and I will not see you as often. After thinking it over and sleeping on it, I realize now what a great honor it is, that my son was chosen as one out of many to continue to still higher education. I am very proud of you. . .and wish you the very best that life has to offer.*

*This is another step forward toward the goal you are seeking. It will be most interesting for you to see how the*

## IX. GROWING UP A MIRAK

*rest of the world lives. . . .We will have a lot to talk about when you get home.*

*Love, Mom.*[1]

Artemis's encouragement had limits, though. When Muriel graduated with honors from Wellesley College with a Fulbright Scholarship to Italy, Artemis probably felt betrayed: after raising three boys, she greeted Muriel's arrival as a kindred soul who would mature as a dutiful Armenian daughter, marry a "nice Armenian boy," reside nearby, and raise grandchildren to be enjoyed. Highly intelligent and strong-willed, Muriel would have none of this and found tranquility only with the Atlantic Ocean between her and Artemis.

But the issue with Muriel was softened by the arrival of grandchildren. And after her two emotional breakdowns, Artemis plunged into painting as a hobby and therapy.

If the emotional interplay between parents and children constituted the main theme in the family's inner life, its adjustment to American society was subordinate but also critical. Mother and father remained faithful to their Armenian identities. Armenian was the language of the home, especially in the early years; and Bob and Sooky attended Armenian language school in late afternoons, or on Saturdays (while their friends were playing baseball and football)—all this despite very old fashioned teaching by immigrant women. Fidelity extended to the church. Infant baptism took place in the newly built St. James Armenian Apostolic church in Watertown, and Easter services were regularly attended. To this day Bob remembers the night time prayer recited in Armenian, *"Hima yes vor bargim bidi,"* "Now I lay me down to sleep."[2] During the war years, however, Bob and Sooky had attended and been confirmed in an Episcopal church in hometown Winchester. Traveling to Watertown each Sunday had been too onerous for Artemis who also had two infants to care for.

As for diet, Armenian food was the staple, although time consuming to prepare. And as in other immigrant households—both Armenian and not—children were expected to play musical instruments, whatever level their talent, or lack thereof. Thus, Bob (violin), Sooky (clarinet), and Muriel (piano). Moreover, as they reached maturity, the children were expected to marry fellow Armenians. To bring an *odar* (non Armenian) into the family was heresy. And in the puritanical atmosphere of the immigrant home, sex education was never discussed.

Visiting relatives—John's or Artemis's adoptive families—on Sundays, usually unannounced, was common. Muriel's vivid, detailed recollections are worthy of note:

## IX. GROWING UP A MIRAK

*As soon as we arrived...the ritual would begin. Greetings were exchanged with kisses on both cheeks among the adults. For us children, the procedure was different, and somewhat painful. Both... [uncles] had the habit of grabbing me by the cheek with index finger and thumb, and shaking my head back and forth,...while repeating, "aghvor aghchig" (nice girl). The smell of tobacco exuded by both...was an added feature of the ritual greeting.*

*At the center of the Sunday gathering was food. Both... [nannies] were accomplished cooks, and set what my mother would call "a beautiful table." Traditionally, Sunday dinner meant roast or grilled chicken, rice pilaf, vegetables (green beans or okra), and mixed salad. After having dutifully emptied our plates, we all withdrew to the living room, where another ritual unfolded. The men (with the exception of my father, an adamant anti-smoker) would sit down and light up their nargiles (water-pipes), or more traditional American cigars, or self-rolled cigarettes, while the women cleared the tables of dishes, and prepared the next act, the dessert. In this interlude, the controversial topics broached at the dinner table were further developed and emotions heated up. As everything was in Armenian, I had little idea of what it was all about. The only frequently repeated phrases I could pick up were "the Turks," "the massacres," the "Old Country," and so on. The nannies had lived through the trauma in Arabkir, while their husbands had been in America*

*There was a large picture hanging on the wall, in both nannies' homes, which showed the figure of a woman, sitting wistfully with her head resting in her right hand, in what looked like a graveyard, amid signs of waste and ruin. This picture, . . . was prominently exhibited. . .in most Armenian homes. Armenia. . .mourning her losses. During these Sunday dinners, the nannies, usually dressed in black, as well as my mother, would end up in tears. They looked remarkably like that figure of Mother Armenia, weeping.*[3]

While the family's inner world focussed on the ancient heritage, the outside world had different ideas and values. In 1939 or 1940 when the family moved to Winchester, the town was overwhelmingly Anglo-Saxon Protestant; the Miraks were one of its first Armenian families and as such constituted an oddity. At school and on the playgrounds, Bob and Sooky were asked why their skins were so dark; their last name was questioned and their diets were considered "funny foods." Embarrassed by his ethnicity, Bob remembers saying his last name was "Smith," and that he was uncomfortable when Artemis spoke Armenian in front

## IX. GROWING UP A MIRAK

of Anglo friends. To be sure, Winchester had a substantial Italian section, but that was on the other, less affluent side of town.

Another theme that coursed through the Mirak household was education. John had graduated from high school and an automotive school; Artemis had left public school to support her surrogate family. But both espoused the values of higher education which they had been denied.

As a young woman, Artemis enrolled "in a correspondence course for adult education, . . . [she] wanted to improve herself for the sake of her children." Accordingly, she was "sent editions of Shakespeare's works, as well as those of other great writers."[4] And as noted above, she relished in reading those great works to her children, often acting out the major roles. John came close to the pure "economic man." But he was ambitious for his children and his mind was protean. For example, as Muriel recalls,

*He purchased a number of important book series, which included a set of at least 25 volumes put out by Walter J. Black. . . .They ranged from Shakespeare to Hawthorne, Cooper and Poe, from Voltaire to Baudelaire, Tolstoy, Dostoyevsky, and Chekhov—the works. Another series was made up of biographies of famous men and women. And for reference, there was a Colliers Encyclopedia. . . .We* were encouraged to join the town library, and to read, read, read—"improve your mind."[5]

Muriel's memories continue: *Father, who would have dedicated himself to studying science, probably engineering or astronomy, imparted to us his love for progress by acquiring the latest technological devices. . . .We had a radio from time immemorial, and he also had a manual wind-up phonograph machine. . . .It could not only play records, but it could also cut them. My father made himself proficient in recording, so that all the important speeches by his hero Roosevelt—the declaration of war after Pearl Harbor, for instance, as well as many of his fireside chats—were immortalized on his 78-speed records. He had cameras of various. . . types as well as a moving picture machine, and a splicer so he could edit film footage. When television was developed, he bought one of the first models. . . .*

She concludes: *Other more spectacular inventions and technological advances were welcomed. . . , especially anything that had to do with space exploration. My father bought a telescope to be able to gaze at the stars, and [in the age of Sputnik and John F. Kennedy] would never miss a feature in the press or on television about space travel.*[6]

## IX. GROWING UP A MIRAK

Duty and devotion to heritage, high expectations, and great aspirations—there were the hallmarks of the Mirak household as its second generation matured. By the Kennedy years, Sooky excepted, Bob, Eddy and Muriel were beginning to move to new households and new challenges.

*Marriages and in-laws.* At age 28 Bob, the first born, was the first to marry. His bride was Alice Kanlian, as expected, a second generation Armenian American. Stunning in appearance (she was called a "Persian princess"), she was a Phi Beta Kappa from Wellesley College, and a promising scientist. However, under societal pressures (few Armenian women of her generation went into professions), she chose teaching, raising a family, and volunteering at high levels. Though sons were expected as offspring, the couple raised two daughters, Julia Christine (1965) and Jennifer Anne (1969).[7]

Alice's parents were well-educated and sophisticated. Her father, Parsegh, raised in Western Turkey and educated in the United States, was an MD who practiced in Chicago. Her mother, Nevart, of a prominent family, grew up and was educated in Constantinople. Striking in her appearance, like her daughter, she prided herself on her part Circassian lineage, renown for its physical beauty.[8]

By contrast, Bob's side of the family—John and Artemis—had roots in provincial Turkish Armenia, Though highly gifted, they lacked the formal graces of higher education; and from this came social frictions—between the well-born and well educated and the talented villager/orphans.

Alice's father passed away in 1963; his widow moved to Arlington, close to Bob and Alice; and the three, with daughters as they came, were a solid troupe. Bob's parents relished in the grandchildren, Julia and Jennifer, and both groups socialized a great deal. But the gap between Alice on the one hand and the in-laws on the other never vanished, a fact which Alice never could accept and for which Bob was occasionally blamed. Sooky, at home with John and Artemis, sided with his parents in their coolness toward Alice. Professionally, Bob, teaching at Boston University was under pressure to publish at the university level while father John wanted his help in the family businesses, especially in the real estate sector. Accordingly, in 1977 he left teaching for the Mirak enterprises. In 1983 he published his revised Harvard Ph.D. dissertation, as *Torn Between Two Lands: Armenians in America, 1890 to World War I,* a volume in the Armenian Texts and Studies series published by Harvard University Press.[9]

Muriel, though the youngest sibling, was the second to marry. In 1965 she graduated from Wellesley College with a Fulbright scholarship to Italy. She settled in Milan, where

## IX. GROWING UP A MIRAK

she received an advanced degree in English literature at the University of Milan and taught there as well as at the Bocconi University. In the late 1970s she shifted her focus from literature to politics and joined the radical organization of Lyndon LaRouche, where she was an editorial board member of their journal *EIR*. In 1973 in Germany she married Webster Tarpley, another highly-educated American member of the organization. Webster, a "Princeton know-it-all," according to Ed Mirak, was not favorably received by Muriel's "down to earth" parents, and his first appearance, bearded and in jeans, in John and Artemis's Arlington home left a poor impression.[10] This marriage to an *odar* (non-Armenian), the first such in the family, lasted two years and ended in divorce, though not because Webster was an outsider. A second marriage, in 1989, to Michael Weissbach, a German member of the organization, took place at the Armenian Cultural Foundation in Arlington, Massachusetts, though the couple established residence in Wiesbaden, Germany, where they live to this day.

Geographically and emotionally distant from the family, Muriel, beginning in the 1980s, gradually bridged that gap by visits home and communications with John and Artemis, a move accelerated by their advancing age and illnesses.

In 2006 Muriel (and later, her husband Michael) broke with the LaRouche organization, and as part of the transition/catharsis process, Muriel embarked on a path-breaking study of genocide and violence especially directed at children in Turkish Armenia, Iraq, and Palestine. Her book was entitled *Through the Wall of Fire Armenia—Iraq—Palestine From Wrath to Reconciliation.* She is currently promoting with vigor efforts to reconcile Armenian and Turkish communities. An authority with many publications on the Middle East, she travels widely and writes regularly for *Global Research, Arab Forum,* and *The Armenian Mirror-Spectator.*

Ed Mirak married in 1974. A graduate of Nichols Junior College in 1963, he served in the United States Air Force Reserve from that year to 1969, with six months active duty in Texas. Learning the automobile business from the ground up—in Mirak Chevrolet's service and parts departments—he headed Ed Mirak Chevrolet in Winthrop, Mass, from 1975 until it closed in 1990, due to Chevrolet Motor Division's restructuring and a poor location. Returning to Mirak Chevrolet in Arlington as its vice president, he became its dealer principal in 2000.

Ed's marriage to Susan Blaisdell was her second. Her son, Robert A. ("Robbie"), was adopted as a Mirak. Susan's

## IX. GROWING UP A MIRAK

father, Robert Blaisdell, was a well-known architect in Greater Boston and a close friend of Johnny Mirak. Susan was an *odar* and a divorcee. But their marriage, now in its thirty-ninth year, and which produced two daughters, Kara and Jessica, disproved the historic prejudices rampant among Armenian Americans that marriages with outsiders and divorced individuals led only to misery.

Charles (Sooky) Mirak, a quadriplegic from the age of 18, found decades-long companionship in Mary Cryan, a nurse from Ireland who was first hired by John and Artemis to care for him during a summer in Maine. The two traveled extensively, something Charlie could never have accomplished on his own. And they spent a number of summers together in Sooky's homes on Lake Kennebago, Maine, and Cape Cod, and winters in Mary's townhouse in Deerfield Beach, Florida. Neurologists credited Charlie's longevity chiefly to Mary's excellent care.

---

[1] Artemis Mirak to Bob Mirak, 1955, in Bob Mirak's personal files.

[2] The familiar child's prayer, which dates from the eighteenth century, reads:

> Now I lay me down to sleep,
> I pray the Lord my soul to keep,
> If I should die before I wake,
> I pray the Lord my soul to take.

[3] Mirak-Weissback, 52-53.

[4] Ibid., 55-56.

[5] Ibid., 59.

[6] Ibid., 60-61.

[7] Johnny Mirak wanted many grandchildren (as well as children). One day he called Bob into his office to ask him when he and Alice planned to have more than their two daughters, Jill and Jennifer. Astonished, Bob replied: "Dad, Alice and I have done our share. Why not put pressure on Eddy and Muriel?" (who were still single). To which Johnny replied, "When a man has four oil wells and three of them run dry, you have to pump the hell out of the fourth." Happily, in a few years, Eddy and his wife Susan brought Johnny more grandchildren.

[8] Circassians, both Christian and Muslim, lived historically in northwest Caucasia and Circassian women, renown for their beauty, were favored by Ottoman sultans for their harems.

[9] Bob's Ph.D. dissertation was directed by the distinguished American social historian, Oscar Handlin. In 1980 Bob also contributed the Armenian entry to the *Harvard Encyclopedia of American Ethnic Groups* (Cambridge: Harvard University Press, 1980).

[10] Interview, Ed. Mirak, Sept. 19, 2011.

## · X ·

# Fin de Siècle
# (2000–2013)

On January 31, 2000, John Mirak, patriarch of the family, passed away at the age of 92. Wheelchair ridden since 1997, when he suffered a massive stroke, he had wanted to die quickly but lingered for three years, in a very unhappy confinement. On his headstone, at his request, was carved: "John Mirak, 1907-2000" and in Armenian letters, "Zaven Mirakian."

Six weeks later, Alice Kanlian Mirak, Bob's wife and John and Artemis's first daughter-in-law, succumbed to cancer, at the age of 59. Diagnosed with breast cancer twenty years earlier, she had undergone a radical mastectomy followed by silicone implants which repeatedly ruptured and created a living hell for her for the next decade and a half, weakening her immune system and allowing the dread cancer to return. In the same year, Alice's mother, Nevart Kanlian, also passed away. Then, in 2003, there were two family deaths: Artemis, the family's matriarch, died of heart failure, age 88 and Betty Mirakian, wife of cousin Joseph Mirakian, passed away. Two years later, Charlie, age 71, died of bladder cancer, a disease associated with his decades-long paralysis. Then, in quick succession, Mary Cryan, Charlie's long time companion, deeply depressed by his death, died, and Taylor Kew, Jill's husband and Bob and Alice's first son-in-law, passed away after a brief but intense struggle against lymphoma. Leaving two young daughters, Taylor himself was just 42.

The pall cast over the family of eight deaths in seven years took its obvious toll. Though the survivors recognized the mortality of the founders who lived into old age, they were crushed by the deaths of a young wife (Alice), a sibling (Charlie), a close companion (Mary Cryan), and a much loved son-in-law just entering the prime of life (Taylor Kew). Was it possible that this was the cruel price paid for the survival of the founders and the family's subsequent commercial success?

In 2002 the family's flagship entity, Arlington Center Garage and Service Corporation, which owned all the family's companies, split into two groups: the Edward Mirak family group and the Robert Mirak family group. The former received the Chevrolet and Hyundai franchises and their real estate and the latter received the rental and

## X. FIN DE SIECLE (2000–2013)

leasing companies and the remainder of the family's real estate holding.[1] Recognizing that the family was moving into its third generation with all the attendant differences in personalities and strategies—indeed, few family businesses survive by the time of grandchildren—Bob led the move to bifurcate. Patriarch John would not have tolerated the split up, staunchly believing that "the boys should stick together." But he had passed away, and Charlie, who also opposed the move, had turned over his reins as dealer principal of Mirak Chevrolet to Ed in 2000 and was removed from the scene. Thus, with the ensuing family deaths, a second profound turn had taken place in the Mirak world.

Looking back from the end of this tumultuous decade, with its schism and deaths, one might argue that the family had lost its bearings and was headed for collapse. After all, could the family overcome the loss of so many members, and would the businesses survive the split up? Clearly, the great older branches had died of old age, and some younger growths had been tragically severed. But there were new, promising offshoots. Ed's family was blessed with seven healthy grandchildren; Bob's numbered four. All were acquitting themselves with distinction. Moreover, the split in the family's businesses surely avoided future rancor and disagreements. And each business entity prospered. Also, the younger generation strove to memorialize the parents' achievements, notably through charitable contributions.

Specifically, Bob and his daughter Jill—aided by a dedicated curator and Board of Directors—continued and expanded the work of the Armenian Cultural Foundation, opening its doors to researchers and the public, through lectures, forums, concerts and publications. Another major contribution was made in Armenia, through the Armenia Tree Project.

In the early 1990s, an independent Armenia endured a war with Azerbaijan, enduring blockades of its borders, and a devastating energy shortage. As a result, Armenians in the countryside and even in the major cities were driven to cut down trees for fuel. The country's forests were being denuded. In 1994 the Armenia Tree Project was founded to reverse these dire trends. In 2008, with funds from the John Mirak Foundation, Bob and sister Muriel traveled to the village of Margahovit in the verdant valley and mountains of Northern Armenia where they dedicated, as part of the Armenia Tree Project, the John and Artemis Mirak Tree Nursery. This was an undertaking soon capable of producing 1,000,000 seedlings a year. The Nursery would also produce jobs for Armenia's many unemployed. In his dedication given to a large crowd in the leafy Margahovit

23. The Mirak family over four generations, Christmas, 1996: Standing from left to right: Susan Mirak (Eddy's wife), Taylor Kew, Alice Kanlian Mirak, Kara Mirak (Eddy and Susan's older daughter), Jennifer Mirak, Eddy Mirak, Jessie Mirak (Eddy and Susan's younger daughter), Michael Weissbach, Muriel Mirak-Weissbach.

Seated: John Mirak, Julia Mirak Kew holding Alex Kew, Charlie (Sooky) Mirak and Artemis Mirak. Missing from the photo: Bob Mirak, and Robbie Mirak (Eddy and Susan's son).

24. Bob and sister Muriel at Margahovit, Northern Armenia, site of the John and Artemis Mirak Nursery.

25. Ribbon-cutting ceremony at the Mirak Nursery. Group includes Rev. Arakel Aljalian, pastor, St. James Armenian Church, Watertown, Mass., Bob Mirak and Muriel Mirak-Weissbach.

26. Memorial stone of the Mirak Nursery.

27. View of Mirak Nursery, which provides jobs for twenty-four people and can produce up to one million seedlings each year for reforestation in Northern Armenia.

valley, Bob said that his father loved mountains, he loved trees and he loved Armenia, and that "wherever they [John and Artemis] are today, they are happy that this project is alive and well." Then in 2013, Bob's daughter Jill joined the board of the Armenia Tree Project and with her younger daughter, fourth-generation Christina she visited the homeland, underscoring their commitment to the family's roots. At the same time donations in the memory of John and Artemis, through the John Mirak Foundation, also flowed to the Avedisian School in Yerevan, Armenia and to the Armenia EyeCare Project.[2] Furthering ties with the ancestral land, in 2012 Muriel and her husband Michael established the Mirak-Weissbach Foundation to help young Armenians in need.

And there were more tributes to the founders. In 2011, under Muriel's stimulus, the Town of Arlington honored the artistic achievements of Artemis with a one-person showing of her art works in the historic Jefferson Cutter House, itself donated by the family to the Town over two decades before.

If the younger generations had thus honored the family's founders and had sunk their own roots, it was still unclear how these Mirak descendants would fare in the future. What would become of them and how would

# X. FIN DE SIECLE (2000–2013)

they succeed? That was for the future to decide. But one thing was clear: the family's foundations, laid by John and Artemis—traced back to Revere, Watertown and Medford, and before that to Mashgerd and Tzack and before that still to the fastness of Dersim—were strong and sturdy, and augured well for all.

---

[1] In the split up of the family's businesses, the Robert Mirak family absorbed Mirak Leasing and Mirak RentACar, and sold them shortly thereafter. The only other Mirak business, Mirak Lincoln-Mercury, Nissan, run by Bob and daughter Jill, closed in 1999.

[2] The Avedisian School, largely funded by Edward Avedisian of Lexington, Mass., in memory of his parents, Khoren and Shooshanig Avedisian, is an ambitious K-to-12 undertaking for disadvantaged Armenians in Yerevan. Its multi-building campus is scheduled for opening in 2014.

Founded in 1992 by Dr. Roger Ohanesian Los Angeles, the Armenian EyeCare Project has evolved into an internationally renown ophthalmology center of excellence. The donation in honor of John and Artemis Mirak is for a retinopathy camera (RetCam) used for detection of diseases in premature children.